A TWEEN BOY'S GUIDE TO PUBERTY

Everything You Need to Know About Your Body, Mind, and Emotions When Growing Up.

For Boys Age 8–12

Abby Swift

BEMBERTON
BOOKS

SOMETHING
FOR YOU

Thanks for buying this book. To show our appreciation, here's a **FREE** printable copy of the "Life Skills for Tweens Workbook"

WITH OVER 80 FUN ACTIVITIES **JUST FOR TWEENS!**

Scan the code to download your FREE printable copy

TABLE OF CONTENTS

1

WELCOME TO THE ADVENTURE

Life is full of exciting twists and turns, and one of the most thrilling rides you'll ever embark on is the journey into adolescence. It's a time of discovery, growth, and transformation that everyone experiences in their own unique way.

To help you understand this fantastic journey, let's follow the story of an 11-year-old boy named Jake.

Jake woke up one Saturday morning feeling a bit different. Over the past few months, he'd noticed his clothes fitting a little tighter and his shoes feeling smaller. And today? As he stretched and yawned, he called out to his pet dog, Max. But instead of the familiar voice he was used to, his voice wavered and cracked unexpectedly, making him sound like a lead singer in a rock band. Was it a dream? Was it his dad playing a prank on him? Nope, it was just Jake experiencing some of the first signs of entering puberty.

Just like Jake, you, too, might notice that things are starting to change. Maybe your voice will crack occasionally. Perhaps you'll shoot up a few inches over the summer or even find a few stray hairs sprouting in new places. It might seem a bit strange and perhaps even scary, but here's the thing: All these changes are totally normal. And believe it or not, they're pretty exciting!

Think of these changes as the beginning of a new chapter in your life. Navigating this chapter can seem daunting, but you don't need to worry — that's precisely where this book comes in! It's like your personal guide, equipped to help you understand and cope with the diverse changes puberty brings.

This book is designed to help you understand and navigate these changes. We've divided it into several chapters, each focusing on a different aspect of puberty. We'll start with the physical changes — the stuff you can see in the mirror, like those growth spurts that might make you the tallest kid in your class overnight or the facial hair that turns you into a teenage werewolf. We'll talk about why these changes happen, what to expect, and how to take care of your changing body.

But puberty isn't just about physical changes. It's also about emotional ones. Ever felt like you're on an emotional rollercoaster, happy one moment and annoyed the next? That's all part of puberty, too, and we've got a whole chapter dedicated to understanding and managing these mood swings.

And that's just the beginning. We'll dive into a wide range of topics, from understanding your changing skin to the importance of good nutrition, sleep, and building self-esteem. Each chapter is filled with tips, advice, and fun facts to help you navigate this exciting time.

Are you ready to embark on this journey? Let's get started!

The ABCs of Puberty

UNDERSTANDING PUBERTY: THE BASICS

Before we embark on this exciting journey, let's start with the basics. What exactly is puberty? Well, puberty is a special time in your life when your body transforms from a child's into an adult's.

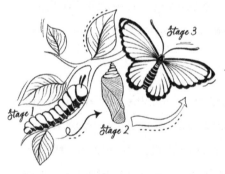

PUBERTY: THE HUMAN METAMORPHOSIS

Think about a caterpillar. It starts its life as a tiny, wriggly creature, munching away on leaves. Then, one day, it wraps itself into a cocoon and undergoes an amazing transformation. When it finally emerges, it's no longer a caterpillar but a beautiful, fully-grown butterfly. This process of change is known as metamorphosis.

Puberty is quite similar. It's your very own metamorphosis. Your body undergoes various changes that prepare it for adulthood, and it's not something that happens all at once. It's a gradual process that takes time. You grow taller, your voice deepens, your emotions become a rollercoaster, and much more. It's a time of significant change and growth, and, just like a butterfly, you emerge on the other side as a transformed individual.

Dealing with the Unknown

This process may seem strange or intimidating, but it's natural and something everyone goes through. Remember, every butterfly was once a caterpillar. And just like them, you're on your way to becoming something extraordinary!

Puberty: Everyone's Journey Is Unique

Puberty is a natural biological milestone and process; every boy experiences it at his own pace. There's no set time or age when it starts or finishes. It's different for everyone, and that's perfectly normal.

Tom and Ben's Story:
Understanding Different Puberty Timelines

Consider two friends, Tom and Ben. They're the same age, go to the same school, and even share the same love for video games. But their bodies decided to start the journey of puberty at different times. Tom noticed his first changes when he was 11. His voice started to crack, and he grew taller than everyone else in his class. But Ben didn't start to notice any changes until he was 13. He was a bit anxious at first, wondering why he wasn't growing as quickly as Tom, but soon enough, he started to see the changes, too.

Their story shows that there's no "right" or "wrong" time to start puberty. It's like waiting for a video game to load. Everyone's Internet speed is different, so some might start playing sooner than others. But eventually, everyone gets to play the game. That's just how puberty works—it starts when your body is ready and not a moment sooner.

Don't worry if you're the first or the last among your friends to start noticing changes. Your body is following its own unique timeline, and that's something to be celebrated!

Now that we know a bit about puberty, you're probably wondering, "What's next? What should I expect?" We're going to take a sneak peek into the amazing transformations your body is gearing up for during puberty.

2

A PEEK INSIDE YOUR BODY

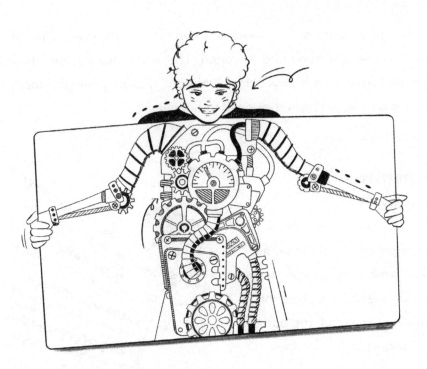

Welcome to the inside story of your body during puberty, where hormones are like the guides of this thrilling expedition. Picture them as dedicated guides, leading the way and delivering crucial instructions from your body's command post to various organs and tissues. Their messages might be simple, but they're incredibly influential: "Grow. Change. Mature."

Testosterone and Estrogen: The Expedition Leaders

Leading the team of hormones are two you might have heard of before — testosterone and estrogen. These two are like the chief guides during your body's transformation. They're giving the main orders for the changes that need to happen.

TESTOSTERONE: THE TRAILBLAZER

Think of testosterone, the principal male hormone, as the trailblazer guide. It's calling the shots, instructing different parts of the body to make specific changes.

When testosterone levels start rising, it's a wake-up call for your body. It tells your voice box to grow, which deepens your voice and may cause it to crack and wobble a bit. It signals for facial and body hair to start growing. It encourages your muscles to become larger and stronger. It even sparks those growth spurts that can make you suddenly taller than your classmates.

ESTROGEN: THE NAVIGATOR

Estrogen, on the other hand, is more like the team's navigator guide. It's primarily known as the main female hormone, but it also plays a crucial supporting role in boys' puberty. Even though it's present in much smaller amounts, estrogen also helps guide growth and maturation in boys.

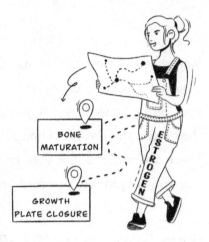

THE PITUITARY GLAND: THE BODY'S EXPEDITION HQ

So, where do these hormones come from? That brings us to a small but mighty gland at the base of your brain — the pituitary gland. Think of this gland as your body's "expedition HQ." Despite being only the size of a pea and being in the base of your brain, it has the colossal task of kick-starting other body parts into transformation.

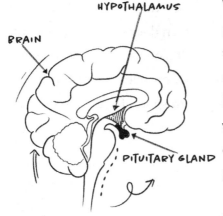

BRAIN

HYPOTHALAMUS

PITUITARY GLAND

When you enter puberty, the pituitary gland knows it's time to start the adventure. It ramps up the production of specific hormones, which then stimulate your testes (the two small oval organs that produce sperm) to produce testosterone.

It might seem like such a significant change would be immediately noticeable, but, in reality, it's a subtle process. You won't feel these hormones zipping through your body. Instead, you'll gradually start to notice the results of their work: the physical changes, the emotional highs, and the lows. These are all signs that your hormones are doing their job, guiding you on your journey to adulthood.

Your Body, Your Timeline

We've talked about the guides of your body's transformation (the hormones) and the expedition HQ directing the action (the pituitary gland). Now, let's look at how the rest of your body responds to the messages they send.

Embarking on the Adventure: Unlocking the Landmarks

As your body embarks on this adventure, think of it as an explorer following an expedition map. Each puberty stage represents a new landmark waiting to be discovered and unlocked. The landmarks correspond to five key stages:

CHILDHOOD (before puberty)

STAGE 1 ♂ 9 - 10 yrs Boys   ♀ 8 - 9 yrs Girls

Characteristics

★ No visible signs of puberty.

* This is the starting point of your adventure, where your body gathers all the necessary tools for the journey ahead..

BEGINNING OF PUBERTY

STAGE 2 ♂ 9 - 14 yrs Boys   ♀ 8 - 13 yrs Girls

Characteristics

★ The breast development and testicular growth checkpoints are unlocked (in girls and boys, respectively).

★ In addition, signs of pubic hair appear, marking another important landmark on your adventure map.

PUBERTY CONTINUES

STAGE 3 ♂ 11 - 16 yrs Boys   ♀ 9 - 14 yrs Girls

Characteristics

★ The journey advances as breasts continue to grow in girls and the penis begins to lengthen in boys.

★ The pubic hair growth checkpoint becomes more prominent as the hair becomes coarser and more plentiful.

ADVANCED PUBERTY

STAGE 4 ♂ 10 - 16 yrs Boys   ♀ 12 - 16 yrs Girls

Characteristics

★ Girls reach the menstruation checkpoint, while boys unlock further genital growth.

★ The highly anticipated growth spurt checkpoint is activated for both.

PUBERTY IS COMPLETE

STAGE 5 ♂ 14 - 18 yrs Boys   ♀ 12 - 19 yrs Girls

Characteristics

★ The final stages of the adventure. Breasts reach adult size and shape in girls, genitals reach adult size in boys, and pubic hair adopts its adult appearance.

★ The growth in height checkpoint slows down and then stops, marking the completion of the adventure.

The Expedition Is Unique for Everyone

It's important to remember that your adventure will look different from everyone else's. Remember our friends Tom and Ben from earlier? Just like their experiences, the timing of these changes varies significantly from person to person.

Let's think of two more friends, Max and Sam.

> *Max started noticing his voice deepening when he was 12 but didn't start growing taller until he was 14. On the other hand, Sam had to adjust to his new height at 13, but his voice didn't start to deepen until he was 15.*

Their stories remind us that there's no standard timeline for these changes. Your body is following its own unique adventure. If you compare your journey to your friends, remember Max and Sam. Just because Sam's height changed before his voice and Max's voice changed before his height, it doesn't mean one of them is right, and the other is wrong. It's all a part of their unique puberty journey.

Like a well-prepared adventurer, your body has its own sense of timing. It knows when it's the right time to start the journey of puberty. Buckle up and trust the process because you're on your way to becoming something extraordinary!

Your Expedition Journal
What's happening on the inside?

As a young explorer on the journey of puberty, keeping a record of your discoveries and reflections is essential. This is your Expedition Journal, where you can jot down what you've learned, ask questions, and document your findings.

> Your Expedition Journal is a tool to reflect on your understanding and experiences. Feel free to share it with someone you trust if you want to.

Use the questions below to help you think about the key points from this chapter.

Remember, your journal is a safe space to express yourself and record your unique experience. There are no right or wrong answers, so be honest and enjoy it!

Explorers and Guides:

What role do hormones play in your body during puberty? Who are the two main hormones mentioned in this chapter, and what roles do they play?

Answer

EXPEDITION HQ:

What is the pituitary gland, and why is it compared
to the "expedition HQ"?

Answer

LANDMARKS ON THE JOURNEY:

Describe the five stages of puberty and the changes
that happen during each stage.

Answer

THE PHYSICAL CHANGES

PUBERTY EXPRESS

COAL

Welcome aboard the Puberty Express! This isn't just any ordinary train; it's a unique ride taking you through the fascinating landscape of adolescence. As we zoom along, each station we stop at represents a different physical change that your body will go through as you head towards adulthood.

Now, while trains usually have stations that come one after another, puberty is more like a high-speed railway with lots of tracks running at the same time. So, even though we talk about "stops" on this journey, many of these changes might overlap or happen in a different order for everyone.

But, no matter the speed or the order of these changes, the goal remains the same: guiding you from the land of childhood to the awesome world of being a teenager.

Fasten your seat belts, look out the window, and enjoy the many transformations ahead. The Puberty Express promises a journey of self-discovery, understanding, and growth. Let's begin the adventure!

VOICE CHANGE: ECHO TUNNEL

First up is Echo Tunnel. The voice box, or larynx, plays the lead role in this act. As the levels of testosterone rise, it signals the larynx to grow. This transformation makes the vocal cords longer and thicker. Like how a bigger musical instrument creates deeper sounds, these changes in your voice box lead to a deeper voice.

This vocal shift usually begins subtly, perhaps as a slight roughness or cracking. You might even find your voice unpredictably alternating between high and low pitches — one moment, it's a trumpet, and the next, it's a tuba. Eventually, as the larynx finishes growing, your voice settles into a consistently lower pitch.

Remember, every symphony follows its unique score, so don't fret if your voice changes before or after your friends'. The musical changes to your voice are a normal part of your body's concert of growth.

Growth Spurt: Skyward Bridge

Next, we arrive at Skyward Bridge, where we unravel the mystery of the infamous growth spurt. This is the time when you might feel like a beanstalk, sprouting taller almost overnight. The growth plates in your bones, under the direction of growth hormones and sex hormones, start their

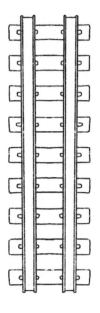

work in earnest. Your arms, legs, hands, and feet might grow faster than the rest of your body, making you feel a bit clumsy or out of sync with your body. This is perfectly normal — it's just your body adjusting to its new proportions, like learning to ride a larger bicycle after outgrowing the old one.

The timing and rate of this growth spurt vary for everyone. Some may experience it earlier, while others might arrive at this destination a bit later. Every timetable is unique, and your body knows your perfect schedule.

FACIAL AND BODY HAIR: THE FURRY FOREST

As the journey continues, your body begins to explore new areas of transformation, including facial and body hair growth. Initially, you might notice a light fuzz on your upper lip or the base of your genitals. This hair is your body's first draft, much like a sketch before the actual painting. Over time, and under the influence of testosterone, this fuzz gradually thickens, darkens, and spreads to other areas, like your armpits, legs, chest, and arms.

The pattern and extent of hair growth vary greatly among individuals, influenced by factors like genetics and ethnicity. Don't be surprised if your body's hair growth story unfolds differently than your friends.

Skin Changes: Oily River

The Puberty Express now takes a turn at Oily River, representing the skin changes you may experience. Stimulated by hormones, the sebaceous glands begin to produce more oil. This increased oil production can lead to acne, especially on the face, chest, and back. Additionally, you might find your skin and hair feeling greasier. Good skincare routines and a balanced diet can help manage these changes.

Genital Development: Hidden Valley

Hidden Valley represents one of the most significant transformations during puberty: the development of the genitals. The testicles are usually the first to grow, followed by changes in the size and shape of the penis. These changes can start as early as age 9 or as late as 14, and can take several years to complete.

Remember, just like with the other changes, the timing and pace of genital development vary greatly. Your body knows its rhythm, so there's no need to compare your changes with others.

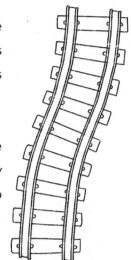

SWEAT CHANGES: FRAGRANT FALLS

Just around the bend on the Puberty Express, we reach Fragrant Falls. With puberty in full swing, your sweat glands are waking up to their new responsibilities. Increased hormones signal them to become more active, leading to more sweat. You might notice this sweat has a stronger smell than before — welcome to body odor!

This isn't something to worry about but rather an indication that it's time to incorporate new hygiene habits into your routine, such as using deodorant and taking daily showers. Remember, this is your body's way of announcing its transition into adulthood.

MUSCLE DEVELOPMENT: POWERHOUSE POINT

As you pull into Powerhouse Point, you'll notice another remarkable change: muscle development. While boys might see a more noticeable increase in muscle mass due to the surge in testosterone, girls also experience strengthening and toning of their muscles, thanks to estrogen and the smaller amounts of testosterone they produce.

This new strength might manifest as an ability to do more physical activities or even excel in sports or other physical challenges. Remember, muscle development varies among individuals and is influenced by genetics, nutrition, and physical activity.

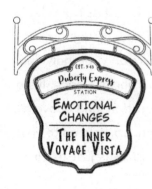

EMOTIONAL CHANGES: THE INNER VOYAGE VISTA

Our final stop is slightly different, as it's more internal than the others. Welcome to Inner Voyage Vista. Although this chapter is about physical transformations, it's essential to remember that emotional and psychological changes are also a big part of the puberty journey.

Hormonal shifts can lead to emotional ups and downs. You might feel more sensitive, irritable, or experience intense mood swings. This is a normal part of the puberty journey and an essential aspect of your developing emotional maturity. Always remember that it's okay to talk about these feelings with trusted adults or friends. You're not alone, and sharing your experiences can make the experience smoother.

As you embark on this journey, it's essential to remember that each bend, tunnel, and bridge we've crossed are a vital part of your unique adventure. While we've described puberty as a series of stops on a train journey, real life isn't always so straightforward. Unlike a train following a strict timetable, puberty doesn't follow a strict schedule or sequence.

In fact, they often tend to unfold simultaneously. Just as trains have different routes and timetables, every person's puberty journey is unique. These changes are signals, and markers on your individual path, showing you're progressing at your own perfect pace. It's a journey of transformation, a journey of exploration, and above all, a journey of becoming the adult version of you. So, hold on to your seat on the Puberty Express because the journey is just as fascinating as the destination!

Your Expedition Journal
What's happening on the Outside?

As you begin your journey aboard the Puberty Express, it's time to add more to your Expedition Journal.

Use the questions below to help you think about the key points from this chapter.

VOICE CHANGE:

What happens to your voice box during puberty, and why does this lead to a deeper voice?

Answer

GROWTH SPURT:

What triggers the growth spurt, and why might you feel clumsy or out of sync with your body during this phase?

Answer

Facial and Body Hair:

Describe facial and body hair changes during puberty. Why might the pattern and extent of hair growth differ among individuals?

Answer

Emotional Changes:

Explain the emotional changes you might experience during puberty. How do hormonal shifts contribute to these changes?

Answer

THE UPS AND DOWNS

As you continue the journey through puberty, you'll find it's not just a physical adventure but an emotional one, too. Like a roller-coaster ride filled with heart-stopping dips and exhilarating highs, your emotions during puberty can take you on a thrilling journey of self-discovery.

In this chapter, we're going to take a closer look at this rollercoaster ride, explaining why your emotions might feel like they're in over-drive and how you can navigate this emotional landscape.

The Emotional Rollercoaster

Why the Ride?

Before we explore the rollercoaster, it's essential to understand why you've been given a ticket for this ride in the first place. You see, puberty isn't just about physical growth; it's also a pivotal time for brain development.

During this phase, your brain is undergoing significant changes. The control center, known as the prefrontal cortex, is responsible for reasoning, impulse control, and decision-making, but it is still under development. At the same time, the amygdala — the part of your brain that handles emotions — is on high alert. This brain renovation means you might experience intense emotions and mood swings.

RECOGNIZING THE UPS AND DOWNS

✦ **JOY:** This is the high point on your rollercoaster ride, where you feel light and exuberant. You might find things that make you happier now more than ever, like hanging out with friends or engaging in a hobby you love.

✦ **SADNESS:** The lows on your ride. It's completely normal to feel sad or down at times. You might feel like tears are a moment away, and sometimes you won't know why.

✦ **ANGER:** This can feel like a sharp, unexpected turn on the rollercoaster. You might get angry quickly and more often. Small things that you used to shrug off might now feel like a big deal.

✦ **ANXIETY:** This is the tight, nervous feeling you get before a steep plunge on the ride. During puberty, you might worry more about your looks, friends, school, or all the changes happening to your body.

✦ **CONFUSION:** Feeling disoriented, as though your rollercoaster took a sudden twist you didn't see coming, is entirely normal. With so many changes, it's okay to feel unsure or confused at times.

THE EXTRA TRACKS

The rollercoaster ride of puberty isn't just about the ups and downs of your emotions. Just like a rollercoaster has different parts—the climbs, the drops, the loops, and the twists—your journey through puberty has different tracks, too. These extra tracks relate to how you think, relate to others, who you are, and how you feel.

THE EXTRA TRACKS

THINKING Differently
Cognitive Development

As you go through puberty, you'll start to think in new ways. You know when you're solving a tricky puzzle or playing a strategy-based video game and have to think hard to figure out what to do next? That's what happens in your brain during puberty. You'll start to think more deeply and ask questions you never considered before. You may question things you've always accepted, form your own opinions, and even think about what might happen in the future based on what you do now.

NEW FriENDS, NEW FEELINGS
Social Development

When you hit puberty, the world of friends and classmates start to take center stage. You might start worrying about what others think about you and want to fit in more. Sometimes, this can make you really happy, but other times, it can make you feel left out or upset.

WHO AM I?
Identity Formation

As you grow up, you'll start to understand more about who you are. You'll begin exploring what you like and don't like, what you believe in, and what role you want to play in your family, school, and community.

FEELING a LOt
Mental Health

Puberty can feel like you've hit the high score on the feeling scale. You might experience many different emotions, and sometimes these can make you feel uncomfortable or upset. These feelings are normal and can be due to the changes in your body, how your brain is developing, and the pressures you might feel in school or with friends. If these feelings become too much, it's essential to talk to someone you trust, like a parent, teacher, or counselor.

Remember, these changes are just part of growing up. Initially, they may seem strange or confusing, but they're all just steps on your journey to adulthood.

You're not Alone

Every grown-up has been on the rollercoaster ride of puberty. They all had different experiences, but no one avoided the ride. Here are some examples:

Meet Jay, who's 11 years old. One day, he was chosen to be captain of the soccer team, and he felt like he had scored the winning goal in the World Cup. But the next day, he missed an easy shot during a game, and suddenly felt like he had lost the biggest game of his life. He felt so low he even snapped at his best friend over a joke.

Then there's Lily. She's always been good at spelling and has never worried about spelling bees at school. But she has felt nervous about even the most straightforward words since puberty.

And then there's Sudip. He's usually as cool as a cucumber — always calm and collected — but lately, he's been feeling angry and confused. The other day, his little brother borrowed his favorite comic book without asking. Sudip got so mad he yelled at him — something he'd never done before.

Remember, recognizing and understanding these emotions is part of your journey through puberty. It's totally normal to feel all of this. And most importantly, it's okay to ask for help when the ride feels overwhelming. You wouldn't try to fix a broken-down rollercoaster by yourself, right? It's the same with your feelings — sometimes, you need a helping hand.

In the next section, we'll look at ways to handle these big emotions, turning the ups and downs into a more manageable and enjoyable journey.

COPING WITH THE HIGHS AND LOWS

The rollercoaster of emotions you're experiencing during puberty can feel intense, but there are ways to make the ride smoother. The first step is recognizing and understanding the changes you're going through.

IDENTIFYING AND UNDERSTANDING YOUR EMOTIONS

- **Pay Attention to Your Feelings:** This means paying close attention to how you feel at different times. Notice when you feel happy, sad, angry, worried, or confused. Try to identify what might have sparked these feelings. Did something happen at school? Did you see or hear something that upset you? How do these emotions change your behavior or thoughts? Paying attention to these things can help you understand your feelings better and give you a sense of control over them.

- **Journaling**: Keeping a journal can help you track your feelings and notice patterns. It's a private space to jot down your thoughts, emotions, and reactions to different situations. What made you feel a certain way? How did you respond? Did you notice any patterns in your reactions or feelings? Over time, you may see patterns, which can help you better anticipate and understand your mood swings.

JOURNALING FOR BEGINNERS

Keeping a journal can be an excellent tool to better understand and manage your emotions. Here's how to get started:

1. **Choose Your Journal:** It can be a physical notebook, an app on a phone, or a document on a computer. Pick what feels most comfortable for you.

2. **Set Aside Time:** Try to write in your journal at the same time each day. It could be when you wake up, after school, or before bed.

3. **What To Write:** There are no rules for this. You could write about your day, describe your emotions, or pen down your thoughts about a situation that bothered you. Here's a simple structure:

   > **Event:** Write about a significant event from your day.
   > **Feelings:** Describe what you felt during that event. Use as many adjectives (describing words) as you want.
   > **Why:** Try to understand why you felt that way. What triggered your feelings?
   > **Outcome:** How did you respond to your feelings? What could you do differently next time?

4. **Be Honest:** Your journal is a safe space to be honest with your feelings. Don't worry about sounding silly or overreacting. Write as you feel.

Once you've started recognizing and understanding your emotions, you can use some strategies to manage them:

Managing Mood Swings

- **Deep Breathing**: This is like a secret power you always have with you. When your rollercoaster car seems to be speeding up, try taking slow, deep breaths. Imagine you're blowing up a giant balloon in your stomach when you breathe in, and let it slowly deflate as you breathe out. This can help slow down your body and mind, helping you to feel more relaxed and in control.

DEEP BREATHING FOR BEGINNERS

Deep breathing can help calm your mind and body when emotions run high. Think of it as pressing the pause button on your rollercoaster ride. Here's how to do it:

1. Find a Comfortable Position: You can sit in a comfortable chair, lie down, or even stand up.

2. Close Your Eyes: This can help you focus on your breathing.

3. Breathe in Slowly: Take a slow, deep breath through your nose. Try to fill your lungs with air. Imagine you're filling up a giant balloon in your stomach. Count to four as you do this.

4. Hold Your Breath: Hold your breath for a count of four.

5. Breathe out Slowly: Now, let the breath out slowly through your mouth, like you're deflating the balloon. Count to four as you do this.

6. Pause: Pause for a count of four before breathing in again.

7. Repeat: Start again, and do this for 5-10 minutes.

Remember, it's okay if you find your mind wandering off. Just gently bring your focus back to your breathing. Over time, you'll get better at focusing and find deep breathing increasingly calming.

- **Physical Activity**: Your emotions are like energy. Sometimes, you might have too much of it bottled up, overwhelming you. Regular physical exercise can help release this energy and balance your emotions.

- **Self-Care**: Just as a rollercoaster needs constant upkeep, your body and mind need regular TLC (Tender Loving Care) to manage emotions. Quality sleep and a balanced diet give your body the energy to navigate the emotional rollercoaster.

TALKING IT OUT

Imagine your emotions are like a backpack filled with rocks. Each rock represents a different feeling or worry you carry around with you. The more rocks you add, the heavier the backpack gets, making it harder and harder to carry.

Talking about your feelings with trusted people — like your parents, friends, teachers, or school counselor — is like taking rocks out of the backpack. It lightens your load, making it easier to keep moving forward.

Don't worry if you're not sure how to start these conversations. It can be as simple as saying, "I've been feeling really angry lately and I'm not sure why," or "I've been feeling really sad and I don't know what to do about it." Remember, it's okay to ask for help, and it's more than okay to take a break when the ride feels too intense.

You're not alone on this rollercoaster ride of puberty, and there are many strategies to help make the journey smoother and more enjoyable. Hold on tight and get ready for the adventure of a lifetime!

Your Expedition Journal
The Emotional Rollercoaster

As you navigate the emotional rollercoaster of puberty, it's time to add more entries to your Expedition Journal.

These questions will help you better understand the ups and downs of this thrilling ride:

Emotional Whirlwind:

Why is your brain like a rollercoaster during puberty? Explain how the changing brain can make emotions feel so intense.

Answer

Navigating the Twists and Turns:

Identify the emotions mentioned in this chapter and explain what they might feel like during puberty. How can you tell when you're riding high or dipping low on this emotional rollercoaster?

Answer

More Than Just a Rollercoaster:

In addition to emotions, what other parts of your life change during puberty? Discuss how thinking, friendships, discovering who you are, and feeling a lot of emotions play a role in the puberty journey.

Answer

Rollercoaster Survival Kit:

What tools can you use to handle the mood swings and intense feelings of puberty? Describe how journaling, deep breathing, and being active can help you manage this wild ride.

Answer

5

THE SKIN YOU'RE IN

As you journey through puberty, you'll notice many changes, especially in your skin. Although your skin is the outside covering of your body, it's important to remember that it's so much more than that. It also plays an important part in your identity, influencing how you see yourself and your self-confidence. As you grow up, your skin changes just like you.

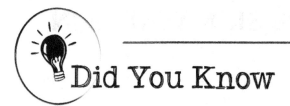

Did You Know

Did you know that the skin isn't just a surface covering? It's actually the largest organ of your body. The skin's surface, if stretched out, could cover about 20 square feet. Its functions range from regulating body temperature and protecting you from harmful microbes to enabling you to feel sensations like heat, cold, and touch.

In this chapter, we'll delve deeper into the changes your skin undergoes during puberty, exploring everything from acne to pores. We'll also provide tips on how to care for and embrace the unique skin you're in.

Pimples, Pores, and More: The Science Behind Skin Changes

As you move through puberty, you may notice your skin changing. This is largely due to your pores, small openings in your skin that allow natural oils, called sebum, to reach the surface. These oils are important for protecting your skin. However, during puberty, hormonal changes can cause the oil production to go into overdrive. The excess oil combines with dead skin cells, creating blockages at the entrances of these small pores.

When these blockages stay hidden under your skin, they turn into a whitehead. But if the blocked pore opens and the contents inside darken when exposed to the air, it becomes a blackhead. Sometimes, natural bacteria on your skin can also get trapped in these blockages. When that happens, it can cause red, swollen spots called pimples or acne.

Understanding these changes can help you care for your skin better during this important time. In the next section, we'll explore some useful strategies for managing your changing skin.

A Simple Skin Care Routine

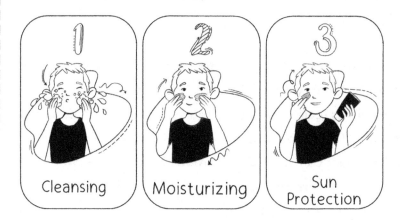

Cleansing   Moisturizing   Sun Protection

When puberty sets in, your skin needs a little extra attention. Here's a straightforward, step-by-step routine to help keep your skin clean and healthy:

Step 1: Cleansing

Cleansing is all about cleaning away the excess oil and dead skin cells that can clog your pores.

You should try to cleanse your face twice a day: once in the morning and once in the evening before bed. Here's how to do it:

1. Wet your face with lukewarm water. Hot water can be harsh on your skin and strip away its natural oils.

2. Apply a small amount of a gentle cleanser that won't block your pores to your fingertips. This is what some people call "non-comedogenic."

3. Gently massage the cleanser into your skin in a circular motion, focusing on areas where you tend to get acne (often the forehead, nose, and chin).

4. Rinse thoroughly with lukewarm water, removing all the cleanser.

5. Pat your skin dry with a clean towel. Don't rub your skin, as this can irritate it.

STEP 2: MOISTURIZING

After cleansing, it's important to moisturize your skin. While it might seem strange to apply a moisturizer when your skin is producing extra oil, skipping this step can actually make your skin produce even more oil.

Here's how to moisturize:

1. Apply a small amount of a non-comedogenic, oil-free moisturizer to your fingertips.

2. Gently massage the moisturizer into your skin until it's fully absorbed.

Step 3: Sun Protection

Finally, protecting your skin from the sun's harmful rays is essential.

1. Apply a non-comedogenic sunscreen with at least SPF 30 to all skin exposed to the sun.

2. Remember to reapply every few hours, or more often if you're swimming or sweating.

ACNE DO'S & DON'TS

DO'S ✓

* **Cleanse Regularly:**
Wash your face twice a day with a gentle cleanser.

* **Hands Off Your Face:**
Avoid touching your face to prevent the spread of bacteria.

* **Stay Healthy:**
Exercise, eat a balanced diet, and sleep well.

* **Use Sunscreen:**
Protect your skin, especially if using acne treatments.

* **Seek Professional Help:**
_ If necessary, consult a dermatologist.

DON'TS ✗

* **Don't Pop Pimples:**
This can lead to scarring and spread bacteria.

* **Avoid harsh Scrubs:**
Use gentle cleansers and exfoliants.

* **Don't Overwash:**
Over-cleansing can strip natural oils and worsen acne.

* **Manage Stress:**
High-stress levels can trigger acne breakouts.

Everyone's skin is different, so you should try a few products before you find what works best for you. Consider talking to a dermatologist or a healthcare professional if you struggle with skin issues. They can provide you with personalized advice and treatment options.

Embracing Your Skin: Self-Acceptance and Confidence

Your skin is as unique as you are. Whether your skin is dry, oily, or a mix of both, it's important to understand and accept your skin type. Hormonal changes during puberty can cause different types of acne, which can be more or less visible and may respond differently to treatments. Embracing your skin, with its imperfections and all, is crucial.

Remember that everyone experiences pimples or skin changes at some point. Your skin is a part of you and your journey, and it's essential to love and accept it as it is.

Be patient with yourself and your skin — changes are a natural part of growing up, and feeling uncertain or self-conscious is okay. With time, you'll learn to appreciate your skin for what it is and find a routine that works for you.

More Than Just Skin: The Importance of Personal Hygiene

In addition to caring for your skin, puberty is a time when overall personal hygiene becomes increasingly important. As your body grows and changes, you'll start to sweat more, and you may notice that your sweat starts to smell different — a bit stronger than before. This is perfectly normal and is caused by the hormonal changes in your body. However, it also means that regular bathing and using deodorant becomes essential.

ALEX'S EXPERIENCE:
BUILDING CONFIDENCE WITH PERSONAL HYGIENE

As Alex entered puberty, he noticed some changes. He began sweating more than usual, and his sweat smelled stronger. At first, he was self-conscious about the changes. He worried that others would notice his body odor, making him uncomfortable at school and when he was out with friends.

Alex's older sister noticed he seemed uneasy and offered some advice. She told him the changes were normal and that he would feel better by showering daily and using deodorant. Alex took his sister's advice.

Showering regularly and using deodorant, Alex became less self-conscious about his body odor and more confident in school and social situations.

Regular Bathing

Showering or bathing regularly is essential during puberty. It helps manage body odor and keeps your skin clean, reducing the likelihood of body acne (yes, you can get pimples on your body, too!). Aim to shower once a day, and always shower after physical activities that make you sweat. Use a mild soap to clean your body, and rinse thoroughly.

Understanding and Using Deodorant

Deodorant is a product designed to mask or eliminate body odor. There are two main types of underarm products that you can use to tackle this — deodorants and antiperspirants.

- *Deodorants* mask or neutralize body odor. They typically contain ingredients that kill bacteria and other odor-causing organisms, as well as fragrances to keep you smelling fresh.

- *Antiperspirants*, on the other hand, reduce the amount of sweat your body produces. They contain ingredients that temporarily block your sweat ducts, reducing the amount of perspiration that reaches your skin.

Whether you choose a deodorant or an antiperspirant depends on your needs. If you're sweating a lot and it's causing discomfort or embarrassment, an antiperspirant may be a good option. If you're more concerned about odor, deodorant could be the way to go. You can also find products that are a combination of the two.

Here's How to Apply Deodorant or Antiperspirant:

Start with clean, dry underarms. It's best to apply these products after you shower when your underarms are free from sweat and bacteria.

Apply the product directly to your underarms. Two to three swipes should be enough if you use a roll-on or stick product. If you're using a spray, a few seconds per underarm is usually enough.

Allow the product to dry before putting on clothes to prevent it from rubbing off onto your clothing.

Everyone is different; what works best depends on your body and needs. There's no "right" choice regarding deodorants and antiperspirants. It's about finding what makes you feel comfortable and confident.

Your Expedition Journal

The Skin You're In

As you explore your skin, let's add some more entries to your Expedition Journal.

The questions below are designed to help you better understand the changes in your skin during puberty and how you can take care of it.

SKIN PLANNING:

What's the role of your skin?

> **Answer**
>
>
>
>

THE SCIENCE BEHIND ACNE:

Why does acne appear during puberty? How do hormones affect oil production and what happens when pores get blocked?

> **Answer**
>
>
>
>

A Simple Skin Care Routine:

Describe the simple routine to help maintain healthy skin during puberty.

Answer

Dealing With Acne:

What are some dos and don'ts when managing acne? Why is it important not to pop pimples or overwash your skin?

Answer

NAVIGATING THE
SEA OF CHANGE

Embarking on the journey of puberty can feel like setting sail across a vast, unpredictable sea. Much like the waves that ripple across the ocean's surface, each individual's experience of puberty is unique and follows its own rhythm.

It's natural for boys to start comparing themselves to others during this time. You might find yourself comparing your height with your friends or wondering why your voice is changing at a different pace. But it's crucial to remember that these comparisons are often unhelpful. Everyone grows and changes at their own pace.

Finding Your Way

This period of change can bring about a sense of pressure. The desire to fit in and ride the same wave as everyone else can be overwhelming. You may wish your body would change faster or slower, comparing your timeline to those around you. However, everyone's puberty journey is different. Your body, growth, and changes are as unique as your fingerprints.

Instead of focusing on everyone else, try directing your attention to your journey. Identify and celebrate your own unique strengths and qualities. You might not be the tallest in your group, but perhaps you're the fastest runner, the best at math, or the most creative in art class. Maybe you're good at making people laugh or have a gift for listening that makes you a great friend. It's important to understand and embrace your unique capabilities and characteristics.

Your Body's Awesome Changes

As you navigate puberty, your body transforms and grows. Each new physical change, from the growth spurt that makes you taller to the deeper voice that echoes when you speak, is another piece that makes you stronger and better prepared for the journey ahead.

However, it's critical to understand that your body is much more than just an object for others to look at. It's far more than the sum of its physical parts — more than its height, muscle mass, or the pitch of its voice. Your body is an incredible tool for life, capable of many activities and experiences.

Think of the amazing things your body allows you to do each day. It enables you to run fast, jump high, play a sport you love, dance to your favorite music, climb a challenging hill, or dive into a pool. Your body allows you to think, dream, learn new things, and solve complex problems. It enables you to create, whether it's painting a picture, composing a piece of music, writing a story, or inventing a new game.

Being Proud of Who You Are

Every person is unique, shining their own beacon of light. Everyone has unique qualities and strengths that make them extraordinary. There is no right way to look or an ideal body because you are more than just your physical appearance. What matters is who you are as a person and how you navigate life.

Just as importantly, your body is how you connect with the world. It lets you feel the sun's warmth on your skin, the taste of your favorite food, the sound of a friend's laughter, and the comfort of a hug. The most important thing is to feel comfortable with who you are and to appreciate your body for what it can do, not just how it looks.

Enjoying the Journey of Growing Up

As you continue the journey of puberty, it's an opportunity to feel good about your body and roll with

the changes that come your way. Remember, you're not just getting bigger and taller — you're changing and growing into the unique individual you're meant to be. Take a moment to think about all the amazing things your body can do. It's the only one you've got, and it's an incredible one at that.

As you ride the waves of change, have fun on this journey, be proud of yourself, and let your fantastic style guide you through this sea of change.

Your Expedition Journal
Navigating the Sea of Change

As you set sail on the vast and unpredictable sea of puberty, let's expand your Expedition Journal.

These questions will help you explore the importance of self-acceptance, appreciating your uniqueness, and building self-confidence during this transformative stage.

STEERING YOUR OWN SHIP:

Why is it essential to focus on your own journey during puberty instead of comparing yourself to others? What are some strengths and qualities you have that make you unique and special?

Answer

BUILDING YOUR SHIP:

How is your body changing and growing during puberty?

Answer

SHINING YOUR LIGHT:

Why is valuing yourself beyond physical appearance important?

Answer

SAILING WITH CONFIDENCE:

How can you enjoy the journey of growing up and feel good about your body?

Answer

THE NIGHTTIME TUNE-UP:
FROM ZZZ'S TO A'S

Sleep is like a tune-up for your mind and body — essential, restorative, and vital for top performance. Think of yourself as a race car on the track of life. As you speed through the day, your engine heats up, and you accumulate wear and tear. Each night, sleep acts as your pit stop, providing repairs and maintenance for your body and brain, ensuring you're in peak condition for the next day.

As you drift off to sleep, your body and brain enter a state of rejuvenation. Your muscles repair, your immune system strengthens, and your brain sweeps away unnecessary information to make room for new knowledge. This nighttime tune-up is crucial for learning, memory, and cognitive performance.

The Mechanisms of Sleep

Just like understanding the engineering of a car can be pretty complex, sleep science is similarly intricate and fascinating.

Sleep isn't just a single state of rest but a dynamic process involving several stages, each with unique characteristics and functions. These stages are categorized into REM (rapid eye movement) sleep and non-REM sleep, the latter of which consists of three distinct phases.

NON-REM Sleep

Non-REM sleep is the beginning of your sleep cycle. It's like pulling your car into the pit stop after a long day of racing and starting the initial checks and repairs.

STAGE 1		Light sleep, is the transition from when you're awake to deeper sleep. Your heart rate slows, and your muscles relax.
STAGE 2		A slightly deeper sleep, is where your body temperature drops and heart rate slows further.
STAGE 3		Deep sleep, is the core of the maintenance process. Your body repairs and grows tissues, strengthens the immune system, and builds bone and muscle. This stage is crucial for physical recovery and growth, especially during puberty.

REM Sleep

After non-REM sleep, you shift into REM sleep. If non-REM sleep is like heavy-duty repairs, then REM sleep is like the detailed fine-tuning of the car for peak performance. During REM sleep, your brain becomes active. This is the stage closely associated with vivid dreams.

REM sleep plays a critical role in mental processing and memory consolidation. This is when your brain reviews and processes information from the day, consolidates memories and replenishes its supply of neurotransmitters, which are vital for brain communication.

Every night, your body embarks on an incredible journey through the stages of sleep, from the initial repairs of non-REM sleep to the fine-tuning of REM sleep. Like a race car getting a comprehensive tune-up, your body and brain undergo necessary maintenance, setting you up for optimum performance in the race of life. Sleep, therefore, is not just about rest; it's about rejuvenation, growth, and preparation for what's to come.

SLEEP PATTERNS DURING PUBERTY

As you become a teenager and navigate puberty, you might notice your sleep patterns shifting. You might start staying up later and sleeping in longer. This shift is a normal part of puberty due to a change in your body's internal clock, known as the circadian rhythm.

It's essential to remember that everyone's sleep patterns are different. Some of us are naturally inclined to be night owls and stay up late, while others are early birds and like to rise with the sun.

Optimal Sleep for Tweens

Experts recommend that tweens and teenagers get about 9 to 9.5 hours of sleep per night for optimal health, mood, and cognitive performance.

While there may be nights when homework or other activities demand your attention over sleep, it's important to remember that cutting back on sleep can be like skimping on a tune-up — it might not show immediate consequences, but over time, it may affect performance.

Just as a well-maintained car is better prepared for the challenges of a race, a well-rested you will be ready for the exciting journey of learning and growing each day brings.

Getting Your Quality Zzz's

It's not just about getting enough sleep — although that's certainly important — but also about ensuring your sleep is restful and uninterrupted. Here are a few practical tips to ensure you get the best sleep possible:

1 REGULAR SLEEP SCHEDULE:
Try to go to bed and wake up at the same time every day, even on weekends. This helps set your circadian rhythm and can make it easier to fall asleep at night and wake up in the morning.

2 REDUCE SCREEN TIME BEFORE BED:
The light from screens can make it harder for your brain to realize it's time for sleep, so try to turn off your electronic devices at least an hour before you get into bed.

3 CREATE A RESTFUL ENVIRONMENT:
Your bedroom should be a peaceful sanctuary for sleep. Keep it dark, quiet, and cool to make falling asleep easier.

You might wonder why we are making all this fuss about sleep. Lack of sleep can make you tired, cause trouble focusing, and even make you sick. Simply put, your body doesn't function as well when you're sleep-deprived.

Getting enough quality sleep helps to keep you on track — it's necessary for optimal performance. By ensuring you're getting enough restful sleep, you're setting yourself up for success every day!

But sleep isn't the only tune-up your body needs for this journey through puberty. Your body also needs nutritious food to grow and develop properly. In the next chapter, we'll explore how to fill your tanks with the right fuel type.

your Expedition Journal
Tuning Up for the Race of Life

As you navigate the fast-paced race of life, let's add to your Expedition Journal

These questions will help you explore the significance of sleep, its effects on your mind and body, and how you can prioritize it during the busy journey of puberty.

In the Driver's Seat:

Why is sleep crucial for physical and mental well-being? How do you feel when you get a good night's sleep, and how does it affect your performance in school or other activities?

Answer

Fine-Tuning Your Engine:

What are the stages of sleep, and how do they prepare you for the next day?

Answer

Pit Stop Priorities:

What challenges may make it difficult for you to get enough sleep during puberty?

Answer

Staying On Track:

What are some practical ways to ensure you get quality sleep?

Answer

FUELING YOUR
GROWTH ENGINE

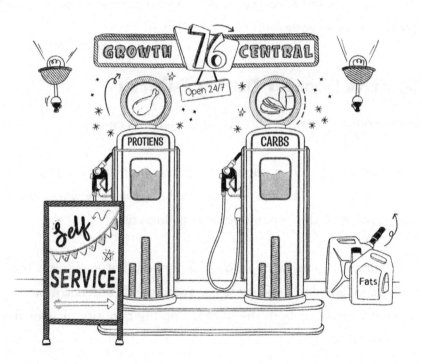

If sleep is your nighttime tune-up, food is the fuel that powers your body's engine. And like any vehicle, your body needs the right kind of fuel to keep it running efficiently. This fuel comes in the form of food, powering everything you do — from solving math problems to playing soccer — and even sustaining the vital processes you might not consider, like the beating of your heart and the growth of your cells.

When a car runs low on fuel, it slows down and eventually stops. Similarly, you may feel sluggish and tired when you don't eat enough or consume the wrong foods. But by fueling your body with the proper nutrients, you can optimize your performance in school, sports, and everyday life.

Appetite Changes During Puberty

During puberty, your body's fuel requirements change.

Feeling hungrier during puberty is normal; your body requires more fuel to grow and develop. As every cell in your body works harder during puberty, the demand for energy increases.

Your hunger is your body's way of signaling that it requires more fuel. It's essential to meet these increased needs with nutritious and balanced foods, as both the quality and the quantity of your fuel are important.

Your Personal Fuel Gauge

You may wonder how much fuel you need during puberty. The truth is the amount varies depending on your age, size, and physical activity level.

On average, teen boys need about 2,500 to 3,000 calories a day, while girls need about 2,200 to 2,400. Of course, these numbers can fluctuate. You might need even more if you're a star athlete or growing quickly.

Remember, these are just averages. Everyone is unique, and so are their nutritional needs. Listen to your body and eat sensibly when you're hungry.

Fueling with Quality: Understanding Basic Food Groups

To support your body's transformation during puberty, it's essential to consume the right nutrients. Let's explore how the basic food groups contribute to your growth and well-being:

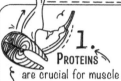

1. Proteins are crucial for muscle growth and repair. Sources include lean meats, poultry, fish, beans, and tofu.

2. Carbohydrates provide the energy your muscles need to function. Whole grains, fruits, and vegetables are good sources of healthy carbohydrates and also contain essential vitamins and fiber.

3. Healthy Fats support hormone production and provide energy for all cellular functions, including muscle activity. Include fats from avocados, nuts, and fish in your diet.

4. Dairy is a source of calcium and protein. Diary products like milk, cheese, and yogurt contribute to strong bones and muscle development

5. Fruits and Vegetables are packed with vitamins, minerals, and fiber, which are vital for overall health. Aim for at least five servings a day from a colorful variety to ensure a wide range of nutrients. Fresh, frozen, canned, or dried—they all count!

6. Vitamins and Minerals such as calcium and vitamin D, are important for bone health.

Understanding these food groups and their functions sets the stage for a healthy and active life, especially during the transformative years of puberty.

Water: Essential for Your Body

Water is vital for your body. It keeps everything running smoothly, lubricating your joints, muscles, and bones and helping transport nutrients. Without enough water, you may experience dehydration, fatigue, and headaches. Aim for about 8 to 10 cups of water a day, adjusting based on activity levels and weather.

A Healthy Plate and Lifestyle

For a balanced meal, visualize your plate divided into sections:

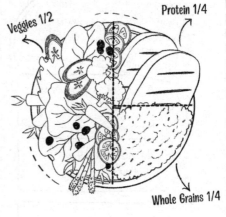

- Half filled with colorful vegetables, like broccoli and carrots (for vitamins and minerals).

- A quarter with a protein like grilled chicken or salmon (for muscle growth).

- The remaining quarter with a whole grain, like brown rice (for energy).

- Accompanied by a glass of water or milk (for hydration and strong bones).

This meal offers a perfect balance of protein, carbohydrates, vitamins, and minerals, giving your body the fuel to hit the track of life at full speed.

SNACKING SMART

While well-balanced meals should provide most of the energy and nutrients your body needs, there may be times when you feel hungry between meals, especially during growth spurts or after physical

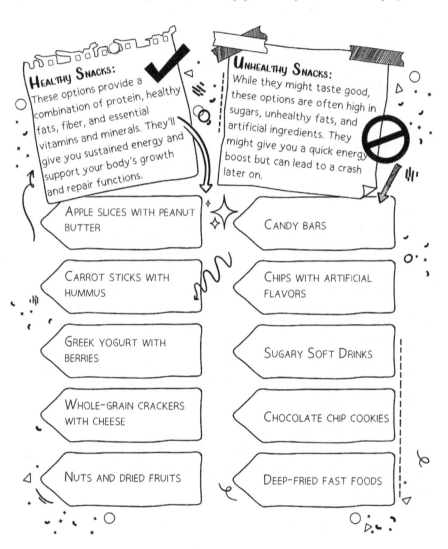

HEALTHY SNACKS:
These options provide a combination of protein, healthy fats, fiber, and essential vitamins and minerals. They'll give you sustained energy and support your body's growth and repair functions.

UNHEALTHY SNACKS:
While they might taste good, these options are often high in sugars, unhealthy fats, and artificial ingredients. They might give you a quick energy boost but can lead to a crash later on.

Healthy	Unhealthy
APPLE SLICES WITH PEANUT BUTTER	CANDY BARS
CARROT STICKS WITH HUMMUS	CHIPS WITH ARTIFICIAL FLAVORS
GREEK YOGURT WITH BERRIES	SUGARY SOFT DRINKS
WHOLE-GRAIN CRACKERS WITH CHEESE	CHOCOLATE CHIP COOKIES
NUTS AND DRIED FRUITS	DEEP-FRIED FAST FOODS

activities. If you need a snack, it's essential to make wise choices that complement your meals rather than undermine them. Here's a guide to help you choose snacks that support your body's growth and development:

CAUTION: THE PITFALL OF UNHEALTHY CHOICES

Like a car filled with low-quality fuel, your body might still be able to run on junk food, but not as efficiently. You'll feel sluggish, have difficulty focusing in school, or even feel cranky. Over time, constantly poor nutrition could lead to weight gain, poor skin, or even serious illnesses.

Don't worry — we're not saying you should give up pizza or your favorite sweets entirely. It's all about balance. By making smart choices most of the time and treating yourself occasionally, you can ensure that your body runs at its best.

YOUR FUTURE, YOUR CHOICES

In this race of life, you're in the driver's seat and have the tools to make your body a champion. As you grow, especially during puberty, keep your engine fuelled with nutritious meals and an active lifestyle. Remember, you're not just building for today but preparing for all the adventures ahead!

Your Expedition Journal
Fueling Up for the Race of Life

As you race through life's journey, it's time to add another entry to your. Expedition Journal with these questions, exploring how food fuels your growth and development.

FueLinG Your EnGine:

Why is it crucial to fuel your body with the right nutrients during puberty?

Answer

UPGRaDeS anD aPPetite CHanGeS:

How have your appetite and food preferences changed since entering puberty? Are there times when you feel hungrier than usual, and how do you respond to these hunger cues?

Answer

Water and Hydration:

How much water do you usually drink in a day? Do you think you're consuming enough to stay well-hydrated? If not, what changes could you make to increase your water intake?

Answer

Snacking Smart:

How do you typically handle hunger between meals? Identify some healthy snack options you enjoy and some less healthy snacks you could replace with better choices.

Answer

THE SPECIAL JOURNEY

Sexuality and reproduction are important and natural parts of human life. As you grow older and go through puberty, your body undergoes various changes that enable reproduction and influence your sexual feelings. It's completely normal to have questions about this. In this chapter, we'll provide some answers to those questions. Let's start with the basics of reproduction.

The Biology of Reproduction

The human body is designed to reproduce, which means making babies. This ability becomes possible during puberty when several changes occur in both male and female bodies.

- **Male Reproductive Organs**: In boys, the testes produce sperm, which is essential for reproduction. During puberty, the testes grow larger, and the body produces more testosterone, a hormone that triggers other changes, like the deepening of the voice and the growth of facial hair.

- **Female Reproductive Organs**: In girls, the ovaries contain eggs. During puberty, hormones like estrogen stimulate changes, such as breast development and the beginning of menstrual periods.

The meeting of a sperm from a male and an egg from a female is the first step in creating a new life. This process is known as fertilization, and it's the beginning of a journey that can lead to pregnancy, birth, and the growth of a new human being.

THe special Journey

Reproduction is how life continues from one generation to the next. In humans, this process involves several key steps:

FERTILIZATION

When a male's sperm meets a female's egg, they can join together in a process called fertilization. This creates a single cell with genetic material from both parents.

EMBRYO DEVELOPMENT

After fertilization, the single cell begins to divide and grow into a cluster of cells called an embryo. This embryo continues to grow and develop inside the female's uterus.

PREGNANCY

Pregnancy is when the embryo develops into a baby. This process takes about nine months in humans. During this time, the baby grows all the necessary organs and body parts, nourished and protected inside the mother's womb.

BIRTH

At the end of pregnancy, the baby is born. This marks the beginning of a new human life, ready to grow and develop like its parents.

PARENTAL CARE

After birth, babies need care and nurturing to grow and develop. This includes feeding, bathing, and teaching, often provided by parents or other caregivers.

These steps might sound complex, but it's a natural and beautiful process that has been happening as long as humans have been on Earth. While understanding the biological aspects of reproduction is essential, there are also emotional and relational changes that you'll experience. Let's delve into these.

Feelings and Crushes

New Feelings

Although we've explored the biological changes during puberty, it's important to recognize that emotional changes are also a big part of this phase. During puberty, you might notice new feelings and attractions and perhaps even experience a crush on someone.

Understanding Crushes

You might find yourself thinking a lot about another person, feeling excited or nervous around them, or even imagining spending time together. It's like having a favorite song you just can't stop playing — it fills your thoughts, and you feel a special connection to it.

These new feelings are a natural and normal part of the changes as you grow up. It's okay to have them, and it's also okay to talk about them with someone you trust if you're curious or confused. As you grow and experience these new feelings, you may also begin to navigate friendships and relationships differently.

Relationships, Respect, and Boundaries

Now that we've talked about different kinds of relationships, let's take a closer look at some key rules that help guide how we treat each other the right way.

Consent and Communication

Consent is essential to any relationship with friends or romantic partners. It means everyone involved agrees to what is happening based on clear communication.

Imagine you and a friend want to watch a movie. You're interested in an action film, but your friend prefers a comedy. You could simply ignore your friend's preference and choose the action film, but that wouldn't be fair or respectful. Instead, you both sit down and talk about what you want to watch, maybe even finding a movie that combines action and comedy. You reach an agreement together that both of you are happy with. This process of discussing and agreeing is consent in action.

The same principle applies to more personal matters. It ensures everyone feels safe and comfortable and respects their feelings and preferences. If, at any point, someone is uncomfortable, they have the right to speak up and change or stop what is happening. Consent is about open communication, understanding, and mutual respect.

RESPECT AND BOUNDARIES

Respect is about recognizing and honoring other people's feelings, opinions, and boundaries, like invisible lines we don't want others to cross.

> Imagine you're building an incredible new LEGO structure. You've been working on it for hours, and it's something you feel proud of. Your friend comes over and wants to add pieces or change part of your design. You're not comfortable with that because this is something personal and meaningful to you. That's your boundary, and it's okay to let your friend know you'd prefer to keep the structure as it is.

In this situation, if your friend listens to your wish and respects your boundary, it helps build trust and understanding between you. If they ignore your feelings and change the LEGO structure, it might feel like they've crossed a line, which can hurt your relationship.

In all friendships and relationships, it's vital to communicate your boundaries clearly and respect others' boundaries. This might include simple things, like not looking through a friend's phone without permission, or more significant boundaries, like needing some alone time. By understanding and honoring these limits, we create a safe and respectful environment where everyone can feel comfortable.

Your Expedition Journal

Navigating the Special Journey

As you embark on the exciting journey of puberty and the exploration of relationships, let's add to your Expedition Journal by reflecting on these questions.

Reproduction Basics:

What changes occur in male and female bodies during puberty that enable reproduction?

Answer

New Feelings:

What emotional changes might you experience during puberty?

Answer

consent and communication:

What is consent, and why is it important in relationships?

Answer

Respect and Boundaries:

What are personal boundaries, and how can they impact relationships?

Answer

10

THE STRENGTH WITHIN

Puberty is a journey with many changes. These changes are not just physical but can also affect how you feel about yourself, view your unique qualities, and interact with others. This chapter is all about celebrating the amazing you and embracing your uniqueness.

Understanding your inner strength and navigating challenges like peer pressure and bullying will help you grow and thrive during this exciting phase of life. Whether it's your sense of humor, artistic flair, athletic ability, or something else, recognizing and cherishing what makes you special is a powerful way to build confidence and resilience.

Building Your Self-Esteem Tree During Puberty

What is self-esteem? This refers to how you feel about yourself, how you see yourself, and your confidence in your abilities.

Like a tree that needs nurturing and care to grow tall and strong, your self-esteem requires attention and support. During puberty, when your body changes and your feelings about yourself may shift, it's a perfect time to tend to your self-esteem tree. By focusing on your strengths and achievements and learning to view your body with appreciation and respect, you can nurture your self-esteem, celebrating the unique and capable person that you are.

Here are some strategies to help you cultivate positive self-esteem and celebrate the amazing you:

Focus on Your Strengths:
Your unique strengths and talents are the roots of your self-esteem tree. Embrace what you're good at, whether it's drawing, playing an instrument, or making others laugh. Let these strengths shine. Your uniqueness is something to be celebrated!

Celebrate Achievements:
Even small achievements matter! Completing a school project, helping a friend, or reaching a personal goal can be celebrated. Think of these achievements as watering your self-esteem tree and nurturing its growth. Each success, no matter how small, contributes to the strength and vitality of your self-esteem, helping your confidence grow tall and strong like a well-watered tree.

Surround Yourself with Positivity:
Just as a tree thrives in the sunlight, your self-esteem flourishes with positive relationships. Spend time with friends and family who support and encourage you. These positive relationships are the sunlight that helps your self-esteem tree blossom, helping you embrace and appreciate your individuality

Nurturing your self-esteem tree doesn't end with recognizing your talents and surrounding yourself with positivity; it also includes embracing and appreciating your body. Your body becomes essential to your identity as you grow and change, especially during puberty. Like every tree's unique shape and structure, every person has a unique body. Getting to know and love your body just the way it is, helps you feel good about yourself. Let's explore some of the incredible aspects of the human body and learn how to view it with admiration and respect.

Embracing Your Incredible Body

Your body is an incredible work of nature, capable of incredible things.

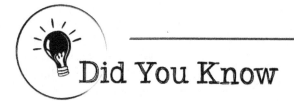

Did You Know

Did you know your bones are as strong as steel but much lighter? Or that your brain can process information faster than the most advanced computer? It's true! Your body is a masterpiece, full of surprises and abilities you might not even be aware of.

Did you know your bones are as strong as steel but much lighter? Or that your brain can process information faster than the most advanced computer? It's true! Your body is a masterpiece, full of surprises and abilities you might not even be aware of.

As you go through puberty, your body will undergo changes, and that's a natural and essential part of growing up. It's easy to compare yourself to others or to images you might see on social media. Still, it's important to remember that there is no "perfect" body. Each body is unique and beautiful in its own way, just like every tree in a forest is different yet contributes to the overall beauty of the landscape.

JAMES'S STORY:
EMBRACING INDIVIDUALITY AND UNIQUE BODY FEATURES

> *Imagine being the tallest kid in your class. That's what happened to James during puberty. At first, he felt a bit weird about it, like he was sticking out from the crowd. But instead of letting it bug him, James decided to make the most of his height. He joined the basketball team and discovered that being tall was actually his superpower! His height was a big advantage on the court, not something to be embarrassed about. Thanks to basketball, James learned to be proud of what made him different. His story shows us that our unique features can be our superpowers!*

Learn to view your body with appreciation and respect, just like James did. Embrace the changes and your uniqueness. Take care of your body by eating well, staying active, and being kind to yourself. Remember, your body is the only one you have and will be with you for all the incredible things you'll do.

Your body should be a source of strength and confidence. Like the self-esteem tree, it needs nurturing, appreciation, and love to flourish. Embrace your individuality, celebrate your body, and let your self-esteem and understanding of your body grow tall and strong. Doing so will prepare you to face whatever comes your way.

Navigating Peer Pressure and Bullying

Just as a tree faces the elements — wind, rain, and storms — you may face challenges from the people and world around you. Peer pressure and bullying are some of these challenges that can shake your confidence and self-esteem. But remember, the strength you've been cultivating by understanding and appreciating yourself is like the tree's deep roots that keep it standing tall.

Resisting Peer Pressure

It's natural to want to fit in, especially when you're growing up. Friends, classmates, and even people on social media might persuade you to think or act in a certain way, sometimes against your own beliefs or values. Peer pressure can sometimes be positive, encouraging you to try new things and grow. But it can also lead to choices that don't feel right for you.

Oliver's Story: Standing Strong Against Peer Pressure

Imagine if someone asked you to skip school to attend a party. What would you do? Meet Oliver, a student who faced that very situation. His friends were all going, and they teased him, saying he was too serious and not fun if he didn't come along. Oliver felt torn, but he knew attending the party wasn't right. It would go against his values and his commitment to his studies.

Like a tree standing firm against the wind, refusing to bend or break, Oliver remained rooted in his values. He courageously and determinedly told his friends "no" and explained his reasons. Though it wasn't easy, Oliver's decision strengthened his sense of self, like the deep roots of a tree that keep it standing tall. He even found that his friends respected him more for his stance. His story illustrates the power of knowing yourself and having the courage to stand strong, even when it's difficult.

The key is to know yourself and your values. Just as you've learned to embrace and appreciate your unique body and strengths, you must recognize what's important to you. It's okay to say no and choose your own path. If something doesn't feel right, don't do it. Trust your instincts, as Oliver did. Don't be afraid to seek support from trusted adults, friends, or family if you feel pressured into something that doesn't feel right.

Handling Bullying: Weathering the Storm

Unfortunately, bullying can be a harsh reality for some, just like a storm that tries to shake a tree. It's a painful experience that can affect your self-esteem and how you view yourself. But remember, bullying is never a reflection of your worth; it's a sign of the bully's insecurities and issues. Just like a storm can sway a tree without uprooting it, bullying is a challenge that can be faced and overcome.

Your unique qualities, positive friendships, and understanding of your own worth are like your tree's strong roots, supportive branches, and resilient trunk. These parts of your tree help you weather the storm of bullying. You might shake, but with the right care, support, and resilience, your self-esteem tree can grow tall and strong.

DIFFERENT TYPES OF BULLYING

Bullying isn't just about physical aggression. In fact, it can take many different forms. Understanding these types of bullying can help you recognize them and take appropriate action. Here are some common types:

1. VERBAL BULLYING:
This includes name-calling, teasing, or making fun of someone. Examples include mocking a classmate for his height or calling someone cruel names.

2. SOCIAL BULLYING:
This involves hurting someone's reputation or relationships, like spreading rumors or excluding someone from a group. An example is starting a rumor that a classmate is not a good friend, leading them to feel isolated.

3. PHYSICAL BULLYING:
This involves harming a person's body or possessions. An example might be a classmate having their backpack thrown in the mud by a bully, ruining their books and personal belongings.

4. CYBERBULLYING:
This is bullying that takes place online through social media or messaging apps. This might include receiving anonymous mean messages about one's appearance on social media accounts.

STRATEGIES TO DEAL WITH BULLIES AND BULLYING

Facing bullying can be incredibly tough, but there are some strategies that can help:

✵ **SPEAK UP:**
If you feel safe doing so, let the bully know that their behavior is not okay. A simple "Stop, that's not funny" can be powerful.

✵ **SEEK SUPPORT:**
Talk to a trusted adult, friend, or family member. You don't have to face bullying alone.

✵ **BE A GOOD BYSTANDER:**
If you see someone being bullied, support them. Sometimes, just being a friend can make a huge difference.

✵ **FOCUS ON SELF-CARE:**
Nurture your self-esteem tree. Continue to embrace your uniqueness, focus on your strengths, and surround yourself with positivity.

✵ **REPORT IT:**
If the bullying continues or becomes more serious, report it to an authority figure, like a teacher or counselor.

Remember, bullying doesn't define you, just like a storm doesn't define a tree. A tree might shake in the wind and rain, but with strong roots and a firm trunk, it remains standing. You're not alone in this, and there are people and strategies that can help you weather this storm, allowing you to continue to thrive and flourish.

Your Expedition Journal
Embracing Your Inner Strength

As you journey through the forest of puberty, it's time to add to your Expedition Journal.

These questions will help you uncover and celebrate your inner strength, discover the value of self-appreciation, and navigate the challenges of peer pressure and bullying.

Planting Your Self-Esteem Tree:

What unique qualities and talents do you have? How can you grow your self-esteem by embracing these qualities and celebrating your achievements, no matter how small?

Answer

Embracing Your Incredible Body:

What incredible things can your body do?

Answer

THE STRENGTH OF YOUR ROOTS:

What values and beliefs are important to you? How can these values and beliefs act as strong roots to help you stand firm against peer pressure and make choices that feel right for you?

Answer

WEATHERING THE STORMS OF BULLYING:

Imagine you or a friend is facing bullying. What strategies can you use to handle the situation and seek support?

Answer

11

IN YOUR CORNER

Life is full of opportunities, challenges, and unexpected twists and turns, especially during puberty. In the game of life, your friends and family are more than just spectators; they're your teammates. They cheer you on, defend you against obstacles, and, most importantly, work alongside you toward achieving your unique goals. Just as a team succeeds by working together and encouraging each other, you too can find strength and success through these supportive relationships.

In this chapter, we'll look at how to build, maintain, and appreciate your team.

BUILDING YOUR TEAM

Everyone needs a supportive team, be it friends, family, teachers, or mentors. Each member plays a unique role, contributing different skills, perspectives, and encouragement. Here's how they function:

FRIENDS

They're out in the middle with you, sharing the highs, lows, and everyday experiences. Good friends understand you, and you can grow, laugh, and face challenges together.

FAMILY

These are the coaches on the sidelines, always there offering advice, care, and unconditional love. They know and care about you deeply and want to see you succeed.

TEACHERS AND MENTORS

They're like the trainers, helping you sharpen your skills and achieve your goals.

YOURSELF

Don't forget that you're the star player! Like any top athlete, you must listen to your coaches and trainers, work hard, and continuously learn and improve. Embrace challenges, believe in your abilities, and lead with determination. It's your game, and your effort and resilience will shape your success and happiness

Emotional Support During Challenging Times

Life isn't always smooth; sometimes, the game gets tough. That's when your team is most important. Friends who listen, family members who comfort, and mentors who guide you all play a different role. They'll lift you when you fall, cheer you on, and celebrate when you triumph. Lean on them, trust in their support, and always remember: In this game of life, you're never playing alone.

SEEKING SUPPORT: OPEN COMMUNICATION

Every successful team has one thing in common: open communication. In the game of life, just as in sports, clear communication with friends, family, teachers, and mentors is key to success. It's how teammates understand each other's positions, intentions, and needs so they can play at their best.

ALEX'S STORY: FINDING STRENGTH

Meet Alex, a young athlete who struggled with anxiety before big games. Instead of bottling up his feelings, he turned to his coach for support. Through being open and honest and sharing his fears, Alex received guidance and encouragement. His coach helped him develop strategies to manage his anxiety and even turned it into a source of motivation. Alex's success on the field grew, and so did his confidence. His story highlights the power of expressing yourself and seeking support.

Whether you're feeling sad, frustrated, or uncertain, learning how to communicate those feelings and ask for help when needed is as essential as any skill. It strengthens your relationships and empowers you and those around you to grow together. Let's explore some strategies to develop this essential skill:

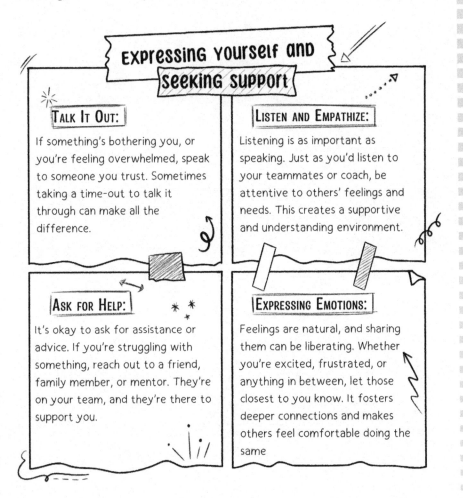

Expressing Yourself and Seeking Support

Talk It Out:

If something's bothering you, or you're feeling overwhelmed, speak to someone you trust. Sometimes taking a time-out to talk it through can make all the difference.

Listen and Empathize:

Listening is as important as speaking. Just as you'd listen to your teammates or coach, be attentive to others' feelings and needs. This creates a supportive and understanding environment.

Ask for Help:

It's okay to ask for assistance or advice. If you're struggling with something, reach out to a friend, family member, or mentor. They're on your team, and they're there to support you.

Expressing Emotions:

Feelings are natural, and sharing them can be liberating. Whether you're excited, frustrated, or anything in between, let those closest to you know. It fosters deeper connections and makes others feel comfortable doing the same

You're Never Alone in the Game

The game of life is not a solo sport. It's a team effort, and you have a fantastic team in your corner. Embrace it, celebrate it, and let it empower you. You're not alone; with your team's support, you're destined for greatness.

Your Expedition Journal
Building Your Team

Let's add to your Expedition Journal.

These questions will help you explore the value of supportive relationships, learn how to communicate with others effectively and embrace your role as the star player in your game of life.

Building Your Team:

Think about the people who support and encourage you. Who are your teammates, coaches, and trainers?

Answer

Your Role as the Star Player:

As the star player of your game, what responsibilities do you have to yourself and your team?

Answer

Celebrating Your Team:

How can you show appreciation for the support and encouragement you receive from your teammates, coaches, and trainers?

Answer

Alex's Story:

What did Alex learn from talking openly about his anxiety with his coach? How does Alex's story demonstrate the importance of being open and seeking support when faced with challenges?

Answer

12

THE NEXT CHAPTER

Growing up is an adventure filled with new experiences, challenges, and opportunities. It's like learning how to ride a bike. You might remember those first few moments, feeling shaky, unsure, and maybe a little scared. But with patience, practice, and persistence, you found your balance, and before you knew it, you were riding like a pro. And the best part? Once you learn how to ride, you never forget.

Looking Forward: Navigating the Future

The same goes for the skills you're learning during puberty. They are valuable tools you'll carry into adulthood, helping you face the future confidently.

During puberty, you discover a lot about who you are. You figure out what you like, what you don't like, what you're good at, and what you want to improve at. This self-awareness will continue to be essential as you make decisions about school, jobs, and friendships in the future.

- **Talking and Listening**: You're learning the importance of expressing yourself and listening to others. These skills are important in all relationships, whether with friends, family, or colleagues. Being able to communicate effectively helps people trust and understand each other.

- **Resisting Peer Pressure**: Knowing your values and standing firm when faced with peer pressure is a lifelong skill. As a teen, you may find yourself in situations where others pressure you to do something you're not comfortable with. Saying "no" and staying true to yourself makes you stronger.

- **Being Yourself**: Just like you've learned to appreciate the things that make you different and special, it is important to continue to embrace what makes you YOU. Whether it's the way you dress, the things you enjoy doing, or the work you want to do when you grow up, celebrate being different.

- **Making Great Friends**: Learning to be kind and understanding helps set the foundation for great friendships now and in the future. Treating others with respect and kindness will always serve you well.

As you continue your journey into adulthood, these skills become the wheels that keep you moving forward. They help you try new things, face new challenges, and celebrate your achievements. Your path might sometimes feel uncertain, but remember your experience with learning to ride a bike. With practice, support, and the courage to pedal, you'll navigate life's twists and turns safely and securely.

THE POWER OF YOU

Your journey through puberty is a crucial chapter of your life, shaping who you are becoming. As you close this chapter and look ahead, it's a time to think about what you've achieved, celebrate it, and get ready for what comes next.

Recognizing Your Resilience:

Think back to the tough times you've faced, the fears you've overcome, and how much you've grown. You've shown incredible strength. You can tap into this strength anytime to help you cope with whatever comes next.

Celebrating Your Community

Think about your friends, family, and mentors who have supported and inspired you. They're a precious treasure. Keep building these relationships, and don't be afraid to make new friends. Together, you'll create a network of support and inspiration that makes your life better.

Looking Ahead With Optimism:

Your journey through puberty is just one exciting part of your life's story. Using everything you've learned, you're ready to take on the future with hope and excitement. Whether it's school, hobbies, or friends, the possibilities are endless.

A Promise to Yourself:

As you move into the next chapter of life, promise to be true to yourself and live with an open heart and curious mind. You can write it down or just keep it in your heart. It's your guiding star that will light your way as you grow and explore.

Your journey through puberty is a big deal, filled with learning, growing, and becoming stronger. It's a celebration of YOU. As you stand ready for what's next, remember how strong, capable, and unique you are.

Take a deep breath, hold your head high, and step forward. The next chapter is waiting, and you're the one who will write it. And don't forget — just as you've learned to handle the ups and downs of growing up, you have the power to handle anything else life throws at you.

The future is bright, and it's all yours. Go out there and grab it with both hands.

Here's to you and the great adventure ahead!

BEMBERTON
BOOKS

THANKS
FOR READING MY
BOOK!

I appreciate you picking this guide to help your tween boy understand and navigate the exciting yet sometimes puzzling journey of puberty.

I would be so grateful if you could take a moment to leave an honest review or a star rating on Amazon. (A star rating is just a couple of clicks away.)

By leaving a review, you'll help other parents discover this valuable resource for their own children. Thank you!

To leave a review & help spread the word

SCAN HERE

Made in United States
Orlando, FL
17 June 2024

47986555R00068